GENDER EQUALITY IN THE SOCIETY

Navigating Inclusivity, Empowerment, And Social Change

Stephanie Bennett

Copyright 2023 Stephanie Bennett

Table of contents

Introduction

Gender equality is a fundamental human right and a key principle for building a just and equitable society. It encompasses equal treatment, opportunities, and requests for individuals of all genders, eliminating discrimination and bias based on gender norms and stereotypes. Achieving gender equality is not only a matter of justice and fairness but is also essential for social progress and sustainable development.

Throughout history, societies have been shaped by traditional gender roles and expectations, often leading to the marginalization and subjugation of certain genders. However, in recent times, there has been a growing recognition of the need to challenge these norms and promote inclusivity, empowerment, and social change.

This comprehensive exploration of "Gender Equality in the Society: Navigating Inclusivity, Empowerment, and Social Change" delves into various aspects of the gender equality movement. It aims to shed light on the importance of gender equality, the challenges hindering its progress, and the strategies required to foster a more equal and inclusive society.

The first section of this study defines the concept of gender equality, setting the foundation for understanding its significance in modern societies. It also offers an overview of historical perspectives on gender inequality, highlighting the progress made so far and the road ahead.

Next, we delve into the impact of gender norms and stereotypes on individuals and communities. By analyzing the influence of traditional gender roles and the role of media in perpetuating stereotypes, we seek to identify ways to challenge and transcend these limiting beliefs.

The legal aspect of gender equality is crucial in shaping policies and frameworks for safeguarding individuals' rights and promoting a fair and just society. This section explores international conventions, national legislation, and the roles of governments and non-governmental organizations in advocating for gender equality.

Education plays a pivotal role in breaking the cycle of gender inequality. Thus, we examine the current status of gender equality in education, access to education for all genders, and measures to address bias and promote equal opportunities in educational settings.

Another key area of focus is the gender pay gap and economic empowerment. We analyze the factors contributing to wage disparities and discuss strategies to achieve economic empowerment for all genders.

Women's representation in leadership and politics is an essential aspect of gender equality. By identifying challenges and encouraging women's leadership, we aim to understand how increased representation can influence policy-making and drive positive change.

Healthcare is an area where gender-based disparities persist. Thus, we explore the healthcare challenges faced by different genders and advocate for improved access to quality healthcare and reproductive services.

Gender-based violence remains a significant obstacle to gender equality. This section addresses the prevalence of such violence, the role of education in preventing it, and the support systems available for survivors and victims.

Recognizing the interconnections between various forms of discrimination, we delve into intersectionality and the importance of inclusivity in the gender equality movement. Collaborative approaches are essential to ensure that no one is left behind in the pursuit of equality.

Furthermore, LGBTQ+ communities face unique challenges concerning gender equality. We discuss the need for inclusivity and the advocacy efforts required to create supportive environments for LGBTQ+ individuals.

Lastly, we explore emerging trends and prospects for the future of gender equality, considering technological advancements, the role of youth, and practical measures for measuring progress.

By delving into these aspects of gender equality, this study aspires to contribute to the ongoing discourse on creating a more just, inclusive, and gender-equal society. Through collective efforts and commitment, we can navigate the complexities of gender equality, empower individuals of all genders, and drive lasting social change.

Chapter 1.

Understanding Gender Norms and Stereotypes

Understanding gender norms and stereotypes means recognizing the expectations and beliefs that society has about how men and women should behave, look, and interact. These norms and stereotypes often dictate what is considered "normal" or "appropriate" for each gender, leading to certain roles and behaviors being assigned to individuals based on their gender. For example, the idea that only men should pursue careers in engineering and women should focus on caregiving perpetuates gender norms.

Stereotypes, on the other hand, are generalized and often unfair assumptions about individuals based on their gender. For instance, assuming that all men are not emotional and all women are not good at sports are common gender stereotypes.

Understanding these norms and stereotypes is crucial to challenging and changing them, promoting a more inclusive and equal society.

Impacts of Traditional Gender Roles

Traditional gender roles have significant impacts on individuals and society as a whole. For example, they limit opportunities for personal and professional growth. When certain roles and occupations are considered suitable for one gender only, it restricts individuals from exploring their true potential and pursuing their passions, like restricting men and women to specific spheres of life, with men typically associated with providing and being assertive, while women are often relegated to nurturing and domestic duties.

Traditional gender roles also perpetuate inequality by:

- Reinforcing power imbalances between genders. Women, in particular, may face discrimination and reduced access to resources and opportunities, while men may be pressured to conform to rigid expectations of masculinity.

Moreover, traditional gender roles can negatively affect mental health, leading to stress, anxiety, and depression when individuals feel forced to conform to societal expectations. The impacts of traditional gender roles can be profound, leading to limited opportunities, reinforced stereotypes, and unequal power dynamics.

By challenging these roles and promoting more flexible and egalitarian attitudes, we can create a more inclusive and fair society where everyone can thrive regardless of their gender.

Challenging Gender Stereotypes

It involves questioning and rejecting the rigid and unfair assumptions about what it means to be a man or a woman. It involves acknowledging that individuals are unique and should not be judged or limited based on their gender.

One way to challenge stereotypes is by

- Promoting diverse and positive representations of different genders in media, education, and other platforms. For instance, showing men as caring and empathetic or women as strong and independent helps break down limiting stereotypes.

Challenging gender stereotypes also means providing equal opportunities for everyone regardless of their gender.

- Creating an environment where people are free to express themselves authentically and pursue their passions without fear of judgment or discrimination.
- Encouraging girls to pursue careers in STEM fields or boys to engage in arts and caregiving challenges traditional gender

norms and promotes a more inclusive society where talents and interests are not confined by gender expectations.

This fosters greater gender equality and creates space for all individuals to thrive based on their abilities and choices.

Media's Role in Shaping Gender Norms

The media plays a significant role in shaping gender norms by portraying certain stereotypes, roles, and behaviors associated with different genders. Movies, TV shows, advertisements, and other forms of media often reinforce traditional gender roles, perpetuating harmful stereotypes. For example, women are frequently portrayed as overly emotional and dependent, while men are depicted as stoic and dominant. These portrayals can influence how society perceives and expects individuals of different genders to behave.

Media representation also impacts body image and beauty standards, with unrealistic portrayals of physical appearance affecting both men and women. By presenting narrow and idealized views of gender, the media can contribute to low self-esteem, body dissatisfaction, and limited opportunities for individuals who do not conform to these stereotypes.

However, the media also has the power to effect positive change by showcasing diverse and empowering depictions of genders. By featuring strong and capable women in leadership roles or men who value empathy and cooperation, the media can challenge traditional gender norms and promote a more inclusive and equal society.

Responsible and inclusive media representation can play a pivotal role in reshaping societal perceptions and promoting a more inclusive and equitable world.

Chapter 2.

Legal Frameworks and Policies for Gender Equality

Legal frameworks and policies for gender equality are rules and guidelines created by governments to ensure that people of all genders have equal rights and opportunities. These laws aim to prevent discrimination based on gender and promote fairness in areas like education, employment, and healthcare. They also address issues like gender-based violence and pay disparities to create a more just and inclusive society.

Some of the key legal frameworks and policies for gender equality include

a. **International Conventions and Treaties:** There are global agreements, such as the United Nations Convention on the Elimination of All Forms of Discrimination Against Women (CEDAW), which aim to protect women's rights and ensure equal opportunities.

b. **National Legislation:** These are laws and regulations enacted by individual countries to address gender disparities within their borders. These laws aim to ensure that everyone, regardless of gender, is treated fairly and has equal opportunities in various aspects of life.

National legislation may cover areas such as employment, education, healthcare, and political representation, to dismantle discriminatory practices and create a more inclusive society.

c. **Gender Quotas:** Some countries implement gender quotas, which require a certain percentage of women to be included in political positions or on company boards, to increase women's representation in decision-making roles.

d. **Anti-Discrimination Laws:** These laws prohibit any form of discrimination based on gender in various settings, such as workplaces, schools, and public spaces.

e. **Equal Pay Laws:** These laws ensure that men and women receive equal pay for equal work, addressing the gender pay gap.

f. **Maternity and Paternity Leave:** Policies that allow both mothers and fathers to take time off work after childbirth to balance family responsibilities and promote gender equality in parenting.

g. **Gender-Responsive Budgeting:** This policy approach ensures that government budgets consider the different needs and priorities of all genders, leading to more equitable resource allocation.

h. **Violence Against Women Laws:** Legislation aimed at preventing and addressing violence against women, providing support for victims, and holding perpetrators accountable.

These legal frameworks and policies are crucial in advancing gender equality and promoting a society where everyone, regardless of their gender, has equal opportunities and rights.

The Role of Government and NGOs in Implementing Policies

The government plays a central role in setting and enforcing laws and regulations to address various social issues, including gender equality, education, healthcare, and more.

- They create policies that aim to promote fairness, justice, and equal opportunities for all citizens, regardless of their gender or background.
- Governments allocate funds and resources to support these policies, ensuring that they are effectively implemented.

- They also monitor and evaluate the impact of these policies to make necessary adjustments for better outcomes.

On the other hand, NGOs (Non-Governmental Organizations) are independent organizations that work alongside the government to address specific social issues and advocate for positive change.

- They often have a specific focus, such as women's rights, environmental protection, or poverty alleviation.
- NGOs play a critical role in bringing attention to important social issues, raising awareness, and mobilizing communities to take action. They often work directly with affected individuals and communities, providing support and services that complement government efforts.

- NGOs also serve as watchdogs, holding the government accountable for implementing policies effectively and ensuring that the needs of vulnerable populations are not overlooked.

However, the government creates and enforces policies to address societal challenges, and NGOs work hand-in-hand with the government to support these efforts, advocate for change, and ensure that policies are effectively implemented for the betterment of society as a whole.

Chapter 3.

Gender Equality in Education

Gender equality in education means that boys and girls, as well as individuals of all genders, have the same chances and opportunities to access and benefit from education. It ensures that no one is discriminated against based on their gender, and everyone can pursue their educational goals without facing unfair barriers or biases.

When there is gender equality in education, both boys and girls are encouraged to study and excel in all subjects, including science, math, and arts, without being limited by traditional stereotypes. Schools and educational institutions promote an inclusive environment where everyone feels safe and respected, regardless of their gender identity.

This also means that everybody will have the same access to education. Access to education for all genders means that every person, regardless of their gender, has the right and opportunity to receive an education. It ensures that boys and girls, men and women, and individuals of all gender identities have equal access to schools, colleges, and other educational institutions. Removing barriers such as discrimination, cultural norms, and economic constraints, access to education for all genders aims to provide everyone with the chance to learn, grow, and fulfill their potential.

By promoting inclusive and equitable education, societies can benefit from the diverse talents and contributions of all individuals, fostering progress and development for everyone.

Addressing Gender Bias in Educational Settings

It means ensuring that boys and girls are treated fairly and equally in schools and classrooms. It involves recognizing and challenging stereotypes and unfair expectations based on gender so

that everyone has the same opportunities to learn and succeed.

To achieve this, teachers and school staff need to be aware of their own biases and avoid favoring one gender over the other. They should encourage all students to participate in activities traditionally associated with both boys and girls, like sports and arts, without judgment or discrimination.

Schools can also provide diverse and inclusive learning materials that showcase positive role models of all genders. This helps break down stereotypes and shows students that they can pursue any interest or career, regardless of gender.

Moreover, it's important to create an environment where students feel safe to express themselves without fear of judgment or bullying based on their gender. This may involve implementing anti-bullying programs and encouraging open discussions about gender equality and respect.

Teachers can play a vital role by challenging gender stereotypes and biases when they arise in the classroom. For example, if a teacher notices that girls are often discouraged from speaking up in class, they can actively encourage them to participate and give their opinions.

Addressing gender bias in educational settings requires a collective effort from teachers, school administrators, parents, and the wider community. By working together, we can create a more inclusive and supportive learning environment where all students can thrive and reach their full potential, regardless of their gender.

Promoting STEM Education for Girls

Encouraging and supporting girls to learn and participate in Science, Technology, Engineering, and Mathematics (STEM) fields. It involves creating opportunities and removing barriers so that girls feel welcome and confident in pursuing STEM subjects and careers.

By doing so, we aim to inspire their curiosity, creativity, and problem-solving skills. It helps girls realize that they can excel in traditionally male-dominated fields and contribute their unique perspectives to advancements in science and technology.

Promoting STEM education for girls can involve initiatives such as

- **Providing Equal Opportunities:** Promoting STEM (Science, Technology, Engineering, and Mathematics) education for girls means giving them the same chances as boys to explore and excel in these fields. It involves creating a level playing field where girls have equal access to STEM resources, courses, and opportunities.

- **Breaking Stereotypes:** One of the essential aspects of promoting STEM education for girls is challenging stereotypes that suggest STEM is only for boys. By encouraging girls to pursue interests in science and math from an early age, we can help break down societal barriers and change the narrative around gender roles in STEM.

- **Female Role Models:** Introducing girls to successful female scientists, engineers, and technologists can be highly influential. Female role models show girls that they too can thrive in STEM careers, fostering confidence and aspirations in these fields.

- **Hands-On Learning:** Engaging girls in hands-on STEM activities and experiments can make learning enjoyable and accessible. Practical experiences help girls build confidence and develop problem-solving skills, making them more likely to stay interested in STEM subjects.

- **Supportive Learning Environments:** Creating supportive and inclusive learning environments is vital for girls to feel comfortable and motivated in STEM classes. Teachers and mentors can encourage participation and guide to ensure girls' voices are heard and valued.

- **Addressing Unconscious Bias:** Educators must be conscious of unconscious biases that may influence their perceptions of girls' abilities in STEM. By treating all students equally and fairly, regardless of gender, girls can thrive in STEM fields without prejudice.

- **Tailored Educational Programs:** Developing educational programs that cater to girls' interests and learning styles can enhance their engagement in STEM subjects. These programs should be designed to foster creativity and critical thinking, encouraging girls to explore STEM in ways that resonate with them.

- **Partnerships with Industry and Organizations:** Collaboration with industries and organizations can expose girls to real-world applications of STEM and potential career paths. Internships, workshops, and mentorship programs can give girls valuable insights into STEM professions.

- **Parental Involvement:** Encouraging parents to support their daughters' interests in STEM is crucial. Parental involvement and encouragement can play a significant role in shaping girls' attitudes toward STEM subjects.

- **Addressing Gender Bias in Textbooks and Curricula:** Ensuring that textbooks and curricula present diverse and inclusive perspectives in STEM fields helps counter gender biases and encourages girls to see themselves as capable contributors to these disciplines.

However, by breaking down barriers, providing role models, and fostering inclusive learning environments, we can cultivate a new generation of girls who are confident and enthusiastic about making their mark in the STEM world.

Chapter 4.

Gender Pay Gap and Economic Empowerment

The gender pay gap refers to the difference in average earnings between men and women. It means that, on average, women earn less than men for doing similar work or work of equal value. This pay disparity exists across various industries and job levels and is often a result of gender discrimination, stereotypes, and societal norms. Closing the gender pay gap is essential for achieving gender equality and ensuring that everyone receives fair and equal pay for their work.

Economic empowerment, on the other hand, means giving individuals, especially women and marginalized groups, the tools and resources they need to have control over their economic circumstances. It involves providing opportunities for education, employment, and entrepreneurship to help individuals achieve financial independence and improve their overall well-being. Economic empowerment enables people to make their own financial decisions, access better opportunities, and have a more significant impact on their lives and communities.

Analyzing the Gender Pay Gap

Several factors contribute to this gap, and understanding them is crucial to addressing and reducing the disparities:

- **Occupational Segregation:** Men and women tend to work in different industries and occupations. Some fields, often dominated by men, offer higher salaries than those typically occupied by women. This occupational segregation leads to variations in pay between genders.

- **Career Progression and Advancement:** Women may face barriers to career progression and advancement, such as limited access to leadership roles or opportunities for growth. As a result, men often advance faster and earn higher wages over time.

- **Work-Life Balance:** Balancing work and family responsibilities can impact women's career trajectories. Taking time off for childcare or family-related reasons may result in interruptions in their careers, affecting their overall earnings.

- **Discrimination and Bias:** Discrimination and bias against women in hiring promotions, and salary negotiations can contribute to the gender pay gap. Unconscious biases and stereotypes may influence decision-making, affecting women's earning potential.

- **Part-Time Work:** Women are more likely to work part-time than men, which often comes with lower pay and fewer benefits. Part-time work can limit their earning capacity compared to full-time employees.

- **Negotiation Skills:** Men tend to negotiate salary and benefits more aggressively than women. This difference in negotiation tactics can lead to variations in compensation levels.

- **Educational Choices:** The fields of study and educational paths chosen by men and women can differ, leading to variations in earning potential in certain professions.

- **Salary Secrecy:** When companies maintain salary secrecy, it can perpetuate pay disparities. Without transparency, women may not be aware of earning less than their male counterparts in similar roles.

- **Unpaid Labor:** Women often bear a disproportionate share of unpaid domestic work and caregiving responsibilities. This can limit their ability to pursue higher-paying jobs or work longer hours.

- **Discrimination Against Mothers:** Mothers, in particular, may face bias and reduced opportunities in the workplace due to assumptions about their commitment and availability after having children.

By understanding and tackling these factors, we can work towards a more equitable workforce where men and women receive equal pay for equal work.

Factors Influencing Wage Disparities

Differences in pay between individuals can be influenced by several factors. These factors can lead to unequal pay for people performing similar work or working in the same job. Let's explore some of the key factors that contribute to wage disparities:

- **Gender:** One significant factor influencing wage disparities is gender. Women, on average, have historically earned less than men for performing the same job or work of equal value. This gender pay gap can result from societal norms, biases, and stereotypes about the roles and capabilities of men and women.

- **Education and Skill Levels:** Wage disparities can also be affected by educational attainment and skill levels. Employees with higher levels of education and specialized skills may command higher salaries than those with less education or fewer specialized skills.

- **Occupational Segregation:** The concentration of men and women in different occupations can contribute to wage disparities. Certain fields or industries may have a higher proportion of men or women, and some of these occupations may pay more than others.

- **Work Experience:** Longevity in a particular job or industry can influence wages. Employees with more years of experience tend to earn higher salaries compared to those with less experience.

- **Negotiation Skills:** The ability to negotiate salaries and benefits can impact wage differences. Some individuals may be more assertive in negotiating higher pay, while others may not feel as comfortable or confident in these discussions.

- **Discrimination:** Discrimination based on race, ethnicity, age, or other factors can lead to wage disparities. Unfair treatment in the workplace can result in lower pay and limited career opportunities for certain individuals.

- **Working Hours and Flexibility:** Differences in working hours, overtime, and flexibility can also contribute to wage disparities. Employees who work longer hours or have more flexibility may have higher earnings compared to those with fewer work hours or limited flexibility.

- **Employer Policies and Practices:** Company policies and practices, such as pay scales, bonus structures, and promotions, can impact wage disparities. Unconscious biases in decision-making processes can also influence who gets promoted and receives higher pay.

- **Economic Factors:** Economic conditions, such as the overall health of the job market, can influence wages. During economic downturns, for example, employers may be less likely to offer significant wage increases.

- **Location:** Wage disparities can vary based on the geographic location of employment. Different regions or cities may have varying costs of living and salary scales.

It is essential to address these factors and create a fair and equitable wage structure that ensures equal pay for equal work, regardless of gender, race, or other characteristics. By addressing wage disparities, we can strive for a more just and inclusive society where everyone's contributions are valued and rewarded fairly.

Strategies for Achieving Economic Empowerment

It means helping people have control over their financial well-being and choices. This is important for everyone, including women and marginalized groups.

Here are some ways to make this happen:

- **Education and Skill Training:** Learning useful skills and getting a good education can open up better job opportunities. When people have skills that are in demand, they can earn more money and have more control over their careers.

- **Equal Pay for Equal Work:** Everyone should be paid fairly for the work they do, no matter their gender, race, or background. This means closing the pay gap between men and women doing the same job.

- **Entrepreneurship and Business Support:** Starting your own business can give you a lot of control over your finances. Providing training and resources to help people start and run businesses can be a way to empower them economically.

- **Access to Credit and Financial Services:** Access to banks, loans, and financial services can help people save, invest, and plan for the future. This can be especially helpful for people previously excluded from these services.

- **Microfinance and Savings Groups:** Microfinance offers small loans to people who want to start or expand a business. Savings groups allow people to save money together and borrow from the group. These can help people build financial stability.

- **Job Opportunities and Workplace Equality:** Creating jobs and workplaces where everyone has a fair chance to succeed is important. This includes offering training, flexible work arrangements, and promoting diversity.

- **Support for Single Parents:** Single parents, often women, may need extra support to balance work and family responsibilities. Offering affordable childcare, flexible work hours, and paid parental leave can make a big difference.

- **Empowering Rural Communities:** Many people in rural areas rely on farming or small businesses. Providing them with better tools, technology, and market access can boost their income and economic independence.

- **Legal Protections:** Laws that prevent discrimination and harassment at work, ensure fair wages, and protect workers' rights are crucial for economic empowerment.

- **Financial Literacy Education:** Teaching people about money management, budgeting, and investing helps them make informed decisions and plan for their future.

- **Digital Inclusion:** In today's world, digital skills are important for economic success. Ensuring everyone has internet access and digital training can bridge the digital divide.

- **Support for Marginalized Groups:** People facing discrimination, such as women, people with disabilities, and minorities, often have less economic power. Offering targeted support and removing barriers can help level the playing field.

- **Community Development Programs:** Investing in local infrastructure, schools, healthcare, and social services can create jobs and improve living conditions, leading to economic empowerment.

By putting these strategies into action, we can help people become more financially independent, make their own choices, and have a better quality of life. Economic empowerment isn't just about money—it's about giving people the tools and opportunities they need to shape their futures.

Chapter 5.

Women's Representation in Leadership and Politics

Imagine a group project where everyone's ideas matter, and everyone gets a chance to lead. That's what we want in real life, too, especially in important places like government and leadership roles. When we talk about women's representation in leadership and politics, we mean having more women involved in making decisions for our communities and countries.

Why Is This Important?

Think about it this way: if only some people get to make decisions, then only some ideas get heard. When women are included, we get a bigger mix of thoughts, experiences, and solutions. Plus, women make up half of the population, so it's only fair that they have a say in shaping the rules and policies that affect everyone.

Challenges to Women's Political Participation

For a long time, there weren't many women in top roles in politics and leadership. Some people believed that only men were fit for these jobs. But that's changing! Many countries are working to make sure women have equal chances to lead. Still, some challenges can make it harder for women to participate fully in politics:

- **Stereotypes and Prejudices:** Sometimes, people have old-fashioned ideas about women's roles, thinking they should stay at home instead of being leaders. These stereotypes can make it tough for women to be taken seriously in politics.
- **Limited Opportunities:** In some places, women might not have the same chances as men to learn about politics or hold important roles. This lack of opportunities can stop women from entering the political world.
- **Unequal Representation:** Many times, there are fewer women in political offices compared to men. When women don't see others like them in power, it can be discouraging and make them think they can't do it too.

- **Balancing Acts:** Women often have many responsibilities, like taking care of their families and homes. This can make it hard for them to find the time and energy to be involved in politics.

- **Lack of Support:** Women might not always get the support they need from their families, communities, or political parties. This lack of encouragement can make it difficult for them to pursue political careers.

- **Discrimination and Harassment:** Some women face discrimination or even harassment when they try to participate in politics. This can make them feel unsafe or uncomfortable, and they might choose not to get involved.

- **Traditional Norms:** In some places, traditional customs or norms might restrict women's roles in public life. These norms can hold women back from participating in politics.

- **Legal Barriers:** In some cases, laws might prevent women from participating in politics or make it harder for them to run for office.

These challenges can make it more difficult for women to have a say in the decisions that affect them and their communities. However, many people and organizations are working to overcome these obstacles and create a more equal and inclusive political world.

Encouraging Women's Leadership in Public and Private Sectors

To get more women into leadership roles, we need to encourage and support them. This means giving girls the same opportunities as boys to learn and grow. It means telling them they can be leaders and showing them examples of awesome women who already are.

It's about creating a world where women have equal opportunities to lead, make decisions, and contribute their valuable ideas and skills.

- In the public sector, this involves promoting and appointing women to roles in government, like being elected officials, ministers, or leaders of public organizations. When women are in leadership positions in the public sector, they can bring diverse perspectives to policymaking, address issues that matter to women and families, and make sure that decisions benefit everyone.

- In the private sector, encouraging women's leadership means breaking down barriers that might prevent them from rising to the top of companies. This can include providing mentorship, training, and equal promotion opportunities. When women are leaders in businesses, they can influence company culture, promote fairness, and bring fresh insights that help companies succeed.

Impact of Women's Representation on Policy Making

Certainly, let's break down the impact of women's representation on policy-making in simple terms:

When more women are involved in making decisions about the rules and laws that govern our society (that's what we call policy-making), some really good things happen:

- **Diverse Perspectives:** Women have different life experiences and viewpoints than men. So, when they are part of policy making, they bring fresh ideas and ways of thinking. This helps make sure that the rules we create are fair and consider different needs.

- **Better Laws for Everyone:** Women often understand the challenges and issues that other women face. When they help make policies, they can make sure that these rules help everyone, especially those who might have been left out before.

- **Health and Education:** Women often focus on things like health care and education. So, having them in policy-making means there's more attention on these important areas, which benefits the whole society.

- **Equality:** When women are at the table where policies are created, it's more likely that rules promoting equality between men and women will be made. This helps to create a more balanced and fair society.

- **Inspiration for Others:** When young girls see women in important roles, like making laws, they feel like they can do those jobs too. This encourages more girls to study, work hard, and aim for leadership roles.

- **Preventing Discrimination:** Women in policymaking can push for rules that prevent discrimination, like unfair treatment based on gender. This makes the society safer and more respectful for everyone.

- **Family-Friendly Policies:** Women often think about family needs. With more of them in policy-making, there's a better chance of creating family-friendly rules like parental leave, childcare support, and flexible work options.
- **Building Trust:** When people see that women are helping to shape the policies, they tend to have more trust in those rules. This trust makes society more stable and peaceful.

So, having more women involved in policymaking is like adding different colors to a painting – it makes the whole picture richer and more interesting. It helps create a society where everyone's needs and ideas are taken into account, leading to better, fairer, and more balanced rules for everyone to follow.

Chapter 6.

Gender Equality and Healthcare

Gender equality and healthcare are like making sure everyone gets the same treatment and care, no matter if they're a boy, a girl, or anyone else. It's about being fair and giving everyone a chance to be healthy.

Imagine going to the doctor when you're sick. Gender equality means that the doctor will listen to you and take care of you, whether you're a boy or a girl. It's not suitable for the doctor to treat you differently just because of your gender.

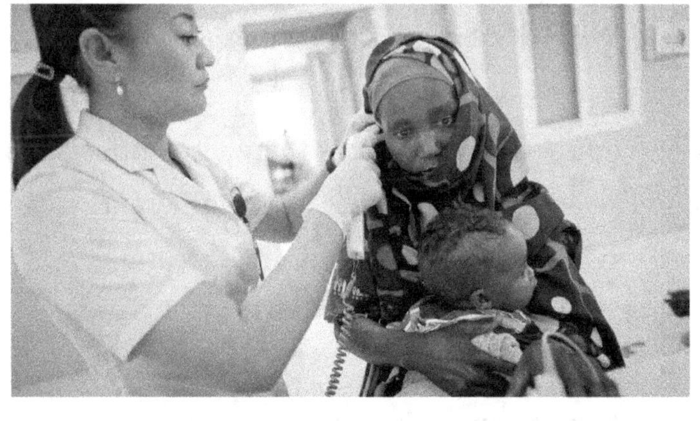

But sometimes, girls and boys, women and men, might not get the same healthcare. Maybe some people think only certain genders need certain treatments, or they might not take women's health problems as seriously. This is not fair, and it can make some people sicker or not get the help they need.

So, gender equality in healthcare is about changing this. It's about doctors and nurses treating everyone the same, no matter their gender. It's also about making sure that girls and women have access to the same medicines, check-ups, and information as boys and men.

When everyone gets the same care, it helps everyone stay healthy and happy. It's like giving everyone an equal chance to have a strong and well-balanced body. And when we all work together to make sure gender doesn't get in the way of good healthcare, it's like building a healthier and fairer world for everyone.

Gender-Based Healthcare Disparities

Sometimes, when it comes to healthcare, there are differences between how men and women are treated. These differences can affect things like how diseases are diagnosed, how treatments are given, and how people's health is taken care of.

One big reason for these differences is that for a long time, most medical research focused mainly on men. This means that some health issues that affect women more weren't studied as much. As a result, doctors might not always know the best ways to treat these issues in women.

Another thing is that people might have some ideas about what's "normal" for men's and women's bodies. This can lead to doctors missing important signs or symptoms in women or not taking their

concerns seriously.

These disparities in healthcare can mean that women don't always get the right treatments or support for their health needs. That's why it's important to make sure that medical research includes both men and women and that doctors understand and consider the specific health needs of women. This way, everyone can get the best care possible, no matter their gender.

Women's Health Issues and Access to Reproductive Healthcare

When we talk about women's health, we're looking at the well-being of girls and women, both physically and mentally. Women sometimes face unique health challenges that need special attention.

One important part of this is reproductive health, which involves everything related to having babies, like pregnancy and childbirth, and dealing with issues like periods and menopause.

Access to reproductive healthcare means making sure that girls and women can get the right medical care and information they need for their reproductive health. This includes things like regular check-ups, family planning, and safe ways to have babies when they're ready.

Sometimes, some barriers can make it hard for women to get the healthcare they need. These barriers might be because of where they live, how much money they have, or even social norms. It's important to break down these barriers so that all women can take care of their health.

Reproductive healthcare is not just about having babies – it's also about making choices that are best for a woman's body and her life. When women have good access to reproductive healthcare, it can help them have healthier lives and make informed decisions about when and how they want to start a family. It's about giving women the power to take care of their bodies and their futures.

Men's Health and Challenging Societal Expectations

When we talk about men's health, we're looking at how guys take care of their bodies and minds. Sometimes, society has certain ideas about what it means to be a "real man," like being tough all the time and not showing emotions. These ideas can make it hard for men to take care of themselves because they might feel like they can't ask for help or talk about their problems.

Challenging these expectations is about changing the way we think. Men need to know that it's okay to ask for help when they're feeling down or stressed. Taking care of mental health is just as important as physical health.

Also, men should know that being healthy doesn't mean they have to be super strong or never get sick. It's okay to go to the doctor and get check-ups. Just like you'd take your car for a tune-up, your body needs a check-up too. Eating well, exercising, and getting enough sleep is good for everyone, not just women.

When we encourage men to talk about their feelings and take care of themselves, we're making sure they have the best chance to live happy and healthy lives. It's like giving them the tools they need to build a substantial house — a house that can handle all kinds of weather and keep them safe and well.

Chapter 7.

Combating Gender-Based Violence

Combating gender-based violence is like standing up against people hurting others because of their gender. It's about making sure that everyone, whether they're a boy, a girl, a woman, or a man, is treated with respect and kindness. Gender-based violence can be physical (like hitting), emotional (like hurting feelings), or other harmful actions. It's sadly quite common, and it happens all over the world, to different people and we're working to stop this and create a safe world for everyone.

Sometimes, people think it's okay to hurt others because they're a different gender or because they have power. But it's not okay. We want to change these ideas and make sure everyone knows that violence is never okay. This is important because when people are hurt, they feel scared, sad, and not valued.

We're doing things like teaching people about respect, helping victims get support, and making laws to punish those who hurt others. Schools, communities, and governments are working together to create a world where everyone can live without fear. It's like building a strong shield against violence, so everyone can live their lives in safety and happiness.

The Role of Education in Preventing Violence

Education is like a powerful shield that helps keep us safe from bad things, like violence. It teaches us how to treat each other kindly and how to solve problems without hurting anyone. When we learn about respect, empathy, and communication, we're less likely to use violence as a way to deal with things.

- In schools, teachers can talk to us about what's right and wrong, and how to treat our friends and classmates with care.
- They can also show us examples of how working together and understanding each other's feelings can make the world a better place. When we know how to talk about our feelings and solve disagreements peacefully, we can stop violence from happening.

- Even at home, our families and caregivers can teach us these important lessons. When they treat us with love and respect, we learn how to treat others the same way.

Education doesn't just happen in classrooms – it's a part of our everyday lives.

When everyone learns about how to be kind, respectful, and non-violent, we build a world where people can live without fear and harm. So, education plays a big role in preventing violence and making our communities safer and happier for everyone.

Support Systems for Survivors and Victims

Support systems for survivors and victims are like safety nets that are there to help people who have been through difficult or harmful situations. These situations could be things like accidents, abuse, or other kinds of harm.

The support systems are like a team of caring people and helpful resources that work together to make things better for those who have gone through tough times.

These systems provide a bunch of things that can help survivors and victims feel safer and stronger. Here are some of the ways they work:

- **Emotional Support:** Talking about what happened can be hard, but these support systems offer a safe space where people can share their feelings without judgment. This can help survivors and victims process what they've been through.
- **Counseling and Therapy:** Sometimes, talking to a professional who knows how to help can be healing. Counselors and therapists can listen, offer advice, and give strategies to cope with the emotional aftermath.
- **Legal Help:** If the problematic situation involves breaking the law or legal rights, support systems can connect survivors and victims with lawyers or experts who can help them understand their rights and options.

- **Medical Care:** For those who are hurt physically, medical care is really important. Support systems can help arrange medical appointments and care for any injuries or health issues caused by the situation.

- **Shelter and Housing:** If someone needs a safe place to stay away from harm, these systems can provide temporary shelter or help find a new, secure home.

- **Hotlines and Helplines:** Many support systems have hotlines or helplines where people can call or text to get immediate help, advice, or someone to talk to.

- **Community Resources:** These systems often know about resources like support groups, workshops, and programs that can help survivors and victims recover and rebuild their lives.

- **Safety Planning:** Support systems can help survivors and victims make plans to stay safe and avoid harmful situations in the future.

The main goal of these support systems is to show survivors and victims that they're not alone and that there are people who care about them and want to help. They help survivors and victims take steps toward healing and rebuilding their lives, showing them that there's hope even after tough times.

Chapter 8.

Intersectionality and Inclusivity in the Gender Equality Movement

Intersectionality and inclusivity are two important keys in the gender equality puzzle. Let's explore them:

Imagine a puzzle with many different pieces. Each piece is a part of who we are – our gender, race, where we come from, and more. Intersectionality is about understanding that all these pieces are connected. It's like a painting where different colors blend to make something beautiful. In the same way, it makes us understand how all these parts of who you are can affect your life. It helps us see that some people might have it harder because they have more parts that make things tough, like being a girl and also being from a certain place.

Now, let's talk about inclusivity. It's like making sure everyone gets a seat at the table. In the gender equality movement, we want to make sure that all kinds of people are included – boys, girls, people of all genders, from different backgrounds, and with different abilities. Inclusivity means nobody is left out, and everyone's voice matters.

So, when we put intersectionality and inclusivity together, it means that we're making sure everyone's unique pieces are seen and heard. It's like making a big, diverse team where everyone works together to make the world fair and equal. When we understand how different parts of our identity come together and make us who we are, we can create a more inclusive world where everyone feels valued and respected.

Recognizing and Addressing Multiple Forms of Discrimination

Sometimes, people can be treated unfairly not just because of their gender, but because of other things about them, too. This is called "multiple forms of discrimination." It's like facing unfairness from different directions.

Let's understand this better with some examples.

→ Imagine a girl who loves to play soccer but she is told that girls shouldn't play sports. This is unfair because of her gender. And if she also comes from a family that doesn't have much money, she might not have proper shoes to play soccer. This is also unfair because of her family's financial situation. So, she's facing discrimination because of being a girl and because of her family's financial situation.

➔ Another example is a boy who has a physical disability and uses a wheelchair. He wants to join a science club, but the club meets in a building with no ramps or elevators for his wheelchair. This is unfair because of his disability. And if he also comes from a different country and speaks a language that's not common where he lives, he might face communication problems. This is also unfair because of his nationality and language.

To help, we need to recognize when this happens and do something about it.

- We can stand up for people who face many types of discrimination and say that it's not right.

- Also, we can make rules and laws that protect everyone and make sure they're treated with respect, no matter who they are.

It means making sure that everyone gets the same chances and opportunities, no matter what makes them different. It's like making sure that the girl has a good shoe and will play soccer irrespective of gender and financial status; and that the science club meets in a place where the boy can easily go.

By working together to stop all these different kinds of unfairness, we can create a world where every person is treated with respect and fairness, no matter their gender, background, abilities, or anything else.

Collaborative Approaches for Inclusive Gender Equality Initiatives

Collaborative approaches for inclusive gender equality initiatives are like teamwork where everyone comes to share ideas to make things fair, learn from each other, and make changes that create a more equal and respectful world for everyone.

These approaches involve people, groups, and even governments working hand in hand to create a better and more equal world.

- **Partnerships:** Different groups, like governments, organizations, and communities, join forces. They share ideas and resources to make sure that everyone's voice is heard, and everyone benefits from the changes.

- **Listening and Learning:** People take time to understand each other's experiences and challenges. By listening and learning, they can come up with solutions that work for everyone, no matter their gender.

- **Education and Awareness:** Sharing information about gender equality and its importance helps everyone understand why it matters. By spreading knowledge, more people become motivated to support equality for all.

- **Policy Changes:** Collaborators work together to create fair rules and laws. These rules ensure that everyone is treated equally, no matter their gender. It's like making sure the game is fair for everyone who's playing.

- **Community Involvement:** When communities come together, big changes can happen. People work on projects that promote gender equality, like workshops and events that celebrate everyone's contributions.

- **Support Networks:** It means creating a safety net for those who need help. It's like friends helping friends when things are tough, showing that everyone cares.

- **Sharing Resources:** By sharing tools, knowledge, and money, everyone can contribute to the cause. This makes the effort stronger and more effective.

- **Open Conversations:** Honest talks about gender equality encourage everyone to express their thoughts and ideas. These conversations help shape better solutions and create a space for everyone's opinions.

- **Promoting Inclusivity:** It's important to make sure that everyone is included, no matter their background or gender. Collaborators create environments where everyone feels welcome and valued.

- **Long-Term Commitment:** Gender equality isn't a quick fix – it's an ongoing effort. Collaborators stick together over time to make sure that the changes they create last and continue to make a positive impact.

Chapter 9.

Empowering LGBTQ+ Communities for Gender Equality

Empowering LGBTQ+ communities is all about making sure that everyone, no matter who they love or how they identify, gets treated fairly and equally. It's like standing up for the rights of people who might face challenges because of their sexual orientation or gender identity. Let's take a closer look at how we can do this:

LGBTQ+ means Lesbian, Gay, Bisexual, Transgender, and Queer (plus more). It's like a big family of different people who have different ways of loving and being themselves. Empowering them means helping them be proud of who they are and making sure they're treated just like everyone else.

Here's how we do it:

- **Respect and Acceptance:** Treating LGBTQ+ people with kindness and understanding is really important. Just like everyone else, they deserve to be accepted for who they are.
- **Laws and Policies:** Making sure that laws and rules protect the rights of LGBTQ+ people is a big part of empowering

them. It means that they have the same rights and opportunities as everyone else.

- **Safe Spaces:** Creating places where LGBTQ+ people can be themselves without fear of discrimination or harm is crucial. These safe spaces can be schools, community centers, or support groups.

- **Education:** Teaching people about different sexual orientations and gender identities helps reduce misunderstandings and discrimination. When we know more, we can be more understanding.

- **Representation:** Having LGBTQ+ people in movies, TV shows, and other parts of media helps show that they're a normal part of our society. It makes them feel seen and heard.

- **Supportive Families:** Families can play a big role in empowering LGBTQ+ individuals. Accepting and loving family members for who they are creates a strong foundation for equality.

- **Advocacy and Allies:** People who aren't LGBTQ+ can also be allies – this means supporting and standing up for LGBTQ+ rights. Advocacy means speaking up for these rights, too.

- **Mental and Physical Health:** Ensuring LGBTQ+ individuals have access to healthcare that understands their specific needs helps promote their well-being.

Challenges Faced by LGBTQ+ Individuals

People who are LGBTQ+ (Lesbian, Gay, Bisexual, Transgender, Queer/Questioning, and more) can face some tough challenges because of who they are. These challenges can make life harder, but we're learning how to make things better.

Let's understand the challenges LGBTQ+ individuals might face:

- **Discrimination and Bullying:** Some people might treat LGBTQ+ individuals unfairly because of their sexual orientation or gender identity. This can happen at school, work, or even in public places. Bullying and hurtful comments can make them feel bad and unsafe.

- **Lack of Acceptance:** Sometimes, LGBTQ+ people don't feel accepted by their families, friends, or communities. This can be tough emotionally, and it can make them feel isolated and alone.

- **Mental Health Struggles:** Because of discrimination and not feeling accepted, LGBTQ+ individuals might experience mental health challenges like depression or anxiety. They need to have support.

- **Limited Legal Protections:** In some places, there might not be strong laws to protect LGBTQ+ people from discrimination. This can affect their rights in areas like work, housing, and healthcare.

- **Safety Concerns:** Some LGBTQ+ people worry about their safety, especially transgender individuals who might face harassment or violence.

- **Coming Out Challenges:** Deciding to tell others about their LGBTQ+ identity (coming out) can be scary. Some fear negative reactions or losing relationships.

- **Misunderstanding and Stereotypes:** People sometimes have misconceptions about LGBTQ+ individuals, which can lead to prejudice and discrimination.

- **Religious and Cultural Conflicts:** LGBTQ+ people might experience conflicts between their identities and their religious or cultural beliefs.
- **Limited Representation:** Sometimes, LGBTQ+ individuals don't see themselves in media or society, which can make them feel invisible.

Advocating for LGBTQ+ Rights and Inclusivity

This means standing up for the rights and fair treatment of people who identify as lesbian, gay, bisexual, transgender, queer, or any other sexual orientation or gender identity. It's about making sure that everyone, no matter who they love or how they see themselves, is treated with respect and has the same rights as anyone else.

Here's how people can advocate for LGBTQ+ rights and inclusivity:

- **Supporting Equal Rights:** Advocates work to make sure that LGBTQ+ individuals have the same rights as anyone else. This includes rights like getting married, having a job, and being treated fairly in all areas of life.
- **Challenging Discrimination:** They speak up against any unfair treatment or discrimination based on someone's sexual orientation or gender identity. They work to change laws and attitudes that hurt LGBTQ+ people.

- **Educating Others:** Many people don't understand what it means to be LGBTQ+. Advocates help educate others about different sexual orientations and gender identities to create more understanding and acceptance.

- **Creating Safe Spaces:** They work to create safe places where LGBTQ+ individuals can be themselves without fear of judgment or harm. This can be in schools, communities, or even online.

- **Using Their Voice:** Advocates use their voice to spread awareness and show that LGBTQ+ rights are human rights. They may participate in rallies, write articles, or share stories to create change.

- **Supporting LGBTQ+ Youth:** Many LGBTQ+ young people face challenges at home, at school, or in their communities. Advocates provide support and resources to help them feel accepted and valued.

- **Working for Legal Change:** Advocates work to change laws that discriminate against LGBTQ+ people. This can involve pushing for new laws or challenging existing ones in courts.

- **Promoting Inclusivity:** Inclusivity means making sure that LGBTQ+ people are included and welcomed in all aspects of society – from schools to workplaces to healthcare.

Building Supportive Environments and Safe Spaces

This means creating places where they feel accepted, respected, and free to be themselves. It's like making cozy spots where everyone can feel comfortable, no matter who they love or how they identify.

Here's how it works:

Imagine a school where students and teachers understand that some kids might have two moms or two dads, and they think that's just as cool as any other family. They make sure everyone can use the bathroom that matches their gender identity, so nobody feels embarrassed. This kind of school is like a safe space.

In a community center, there might be groups where LGBTQ+ people can meet, share their stories, and support each other. It's a bit like a clubhouse where they know they belong, and nobody will judge them. This is a supportive environment.

Online, there are websites and social media groups where LGBTQ+ folks can connect with others who get what they're going through. It's like a big virtual hangout where they can be themselves without worrying about mean comments.

Supportive environments and safe spaces can be anywhere — schools, homes, community centers, and even online spaces. They show that everyone deserves to be treated with kindness and respect, no matter who they are. It's about making the world a better, more understanding place for everyone.

Chapter 10.

The Future of Gender Equality: Emerging Trends and Prospects

Looking ahead to the future of gender equality, we can see some exciting changes and possibilities. Let's explore what's coming:

In the future, we are likely to see more people working together to make sure that everyone is treated fairly, no matter their gender. This means that boys and girls, men and women, and people of all genders will have the same opportunities and chances to succeed in life.

We might also notice more people understanding that gender isn't just about being a boy or a girl. Some people might not feel like they fit into these categories, and that's okay. The future might bring more acceptance and respect for people who are different and don't fit into traditional ideas about gender.

Technology is going to play a big role too. New inventions might help girls and boys learn and study the same things, and women and men might have equal access to jobs that were once seen as just for one gender. Technology could also make it easier for people to connect and share their ideas about gender equality all around the world.

It's important to remember that the future of gender equality isn't just about laws and rules. It's also about changing the way people think and feel. This means families, schools, communities, and governments will all need to work together to make sure everyone is treated fairly and respectfully, no matter their gender.

Technological Advancements and Gender Equality

Technology is like a big toolbox that can help make the world more fair for everyone. Let's see how new inventions and ideas can help with gender equality:

- Technology can spread information quickly. This means we can learn about what's fair and what's not, and tell everyone. For example, we can use social media to share stories and ideas about treating boys and girls the same.

- With technology, we can talk to people far away. This helps us work together even if we're not in the same place. We can talk about gender equality with people from different countries and learn from each other.

- Sometimes, people use technology to do unfair things, like saying mean things online. But we're also learning how to use technology to stop this and create safe places on the internet.

Technology is like a superpower that can help make sure everyone is treated fairly. We use it to learn, share ideas, and work together. It's like a tool that helps us build a world where everyone is equal and respected.

Youth and the Next Generation of Change

Young people are like the superheroes of the future when it comes to making the world better and more equal. They have fresh ideas, energy, and a big desire to create positive changes.

Let's look at how youth can shape the next generation of change:

- **Young Minds, Big Ideas:**
Young people see the world with new eyes. They're not used to doing things a certain way just because that's how it's always been done. This means they can come up with creative ideas that might solve problems better. When they bring their ideas to the table, they're like a breath of fresh air.

- **Tech-Savvy Power:**

Youth are usually really good with technology, and they know how to use it to spread messages and connect with others. This power can be used to raise awareness about important issues, organize events, and even start movements for change. Technology makes their voices even stronger.

- **Passion for Justice:**

Young people often have strong feelings about what's right and fair. They don't like seeing anyone treated unfairly. This passion can fuel their efforts to stand up for gender equality and other important causes. When they join together, their passion can create a big impact.

- **Changing Attitudes:**

As young people learn about gender equality and fairness, they can share these ideas with their families, friends, and communities. This creates a ripple effect, where more and more people start to understand the importance of treating everyone equally, no matter their gender.

- **Leaders of Tomorrow:**

Today's youth are tomorrow's leaders. They're learning important skills now that will help them become the decision-makers of the future. When they learn about gender equality from a young age, they grow up knowing that it's a normal and necessary part of life.

Measuring Progress and Charting the Path Ahead

Measuring progress and charting the path ahead for gender equality is like using a map to see how far we've come and where we want to go.

For example:

Imagine you're on a journey to make sure that all your friends can play with the same toys at school. First, you might count how many toys are for boys and how many are for girls. This helps you see if things are fair or if one group has more toys than the other.

Then, you might ask your friends how they feel about the toys. Are they happy? Do they think it's fair? This helps you understand if everyone is treated equally and if any changes are needed.

As time goes by, you might check again to see if more toys are being shared equally. If things are getting better, it's like a sign that your journey is working. But if things stay the same, you know you need to keep trying.

Just like this, with gender equality, we use numbers, stories, and feedback to see if boys and girls, men and women, are being treated fairly. We look at things like how many girls go to school, how many women have important jobs, and if anyone is treated differently because of their gender.

If more girls go to school or more women become leaders, it means we're making progress. But if we still see differences, we know there's more work to do. This helps us plan what steps to take next, like making sure everyone has the same opportunities to learn and lead.

So, measuring progress and charting the path ahead is like keeping an eye on the journey toward fairness and using what we learn to make the road smoother for everyone. It's all about making sure that everyone, no matter who they are, has a fair and happy future.

Conclusion

To sum it all up, gender equality is like making sure that everyone, whether they're a boy, a girl, a man, or a woman, is treated fairly and with respect. It's about breaking old ideas that say some people should have more rights or chances just because of their gender.

We've talked about a lot of important things in this journey towards fairness. From understanding gender roles and stereotypes to promoting education for all genders, from tackling the gender pay gap to empowering LGBTQ+ communities, and from involving men as allies to using technology for a better future – every step is a part of this big puzzle of equality.

Remember, it's not just a fight for one group; it's a fight for all of us. The future holds exciting possibilities with young voices leading the way and technology helping us be even fairer. By supporting each other, standing up for what's right, and making sure everyone's voice is heard, we can create a world where everyone's uniqueness is celebrated and respected. Together, we can make sure that gender equality is not just a dream, but a reality for everyone.

Call to Action for Advancing Gender Equality in Society

Here's how we can all work together to make things fairer for everyone, no matter their gender:

- **Respect Everyone:** Treat every person kindly and with respect, no matter if they're a boy, a girl, a man, or a woman. Fairness starts with how we treat each other.

- **Speak Up:** If you see something that's not fair like someone being bullied or treated badly because of their gender, don't be afraid to speak up. Our voices are powerful.

- **Learn and Teach:** Educate yourself about gender equality and share what you learn with others. The more people know, the better we can all make the world.

- **Support Change:** Support organizations and initiatives that work for gender equality. Even small actions, like attending events or sharing messages, can make a big difference.

- **Be a Role Model:** Show others how to be fair and kind. Be someone who treats everyone equally and stands up for what's right.

- **Challenge Stereotypes:** Don't believe in stereotypes that say how boys and girls should act. Be yourself, and let others be themselves too.

- **Listen and Learn:** Listen to people's experiences and stories. Learning from each other helps us create a world that's better for everyone.
- **Encourage Equality:** Encourage your family, friends, and community to treat everyone fairly. Our combined efforts can bring big changes.
- **Support Each Other:** Support people who've faced discrimination or challenges because of their gender. Together, we can make sure everyone feels strong and valued.
- **Believe in Change:** Believe that we can create a world where everyone has the same opportunities, no matter their gender. Our actions today shape a better tomorrow.

We can speak up, learn, and support change to make the world better for all genders. By being role models, challenging stereotypes, and listening to each other, we create a future where equality is the norm. Let's believe in this change and take action today for a brighter tomorrow.